Frontispiece *In the streets of Leon, members of the FSLN, the Sandinista Front for National Liberation, fight to keep the city from the National Guard the force keeping Anastasio Somoza in power.*

THE CRISIS
IN CENTRAL
AMERICA

John Griffiths

Wayland

The Conflict in Afghanistan   The Revolution in Iran
The Arab-Israeli Issue   The Irish Question
The Division of Berlin   The Korean War
The Crisis in Central America   The Libyan Question
The Cuban Missile Crisis   The Rise of Solidarity
The Falklands Conflict   The Crisis in South Africa
The Gulf War   The Suez Crisis
The Hungarian Uprising   The Vietnam War
The Partition of India

Consultant: Marigold Best, Secretary Latin
America Committee, Quaker Peace &
Service (in her personal capacity).

Author: John Griffiths, Senior Lecturer in Caribbean,
Cuban and Latin American history, at the Polytechnic of North London.

Editor: Hazel Songhurst

British Library Cataloguing in Publication Data

Griffiths, John, *1942 Apr 5-*
   The crisis in Central America.—(Flashpoints).
   1. Central America — Politics and government — 1979–
   I. Title   II. Series
   972.8′053   F1439.5

ISBN 1-85210-302-7

Typeset, printed and bound in Great Britain at The Bath Press, Avon

Contents

1
The entry of the FSLN into Managua

'I'll neither go nor be driven out ...' (Anastasio Somoza Debayle, November 1978).

19 July, 1979; everyone seemed to be out on the streets of Managua, Nicaragua's capital city. It was like a carnival. Thousands of young rebels, most of them in the olive green uniforms of the FSLN, the Sandinista Front for National Liberation, drove around the city waving the black and red flag of the Sandinistas and firing shots in the air. Some had immediately taken control of Somoza's 'Bunker', the deposed President's military headquarters, seizing hundreds of weapons which had been supplied by the United States in a last ditch attempt to keep the Sandinistas from power. Dozens of political prisoners were enjoying freedom for the first time in years. Many had been cruelly tortured by Somoza's National Guard, who were now themselves in custody. There were reports of National Guards fleeing the country to escape the retribution of the people, just as Somoza himself had done two days before. FSLN commanders were already taking on the responsibility of government; two of them were sifting through what was left of Somoza's files. Outside Managua, cheering crowds pulled down a statue of the deposed President's father, Anastasio Somoza Garcia, who had founded the Somoza family dynasty over four decades before.

In the streets families were looking out for sons and daughters who had joined the ranks of the FSLN many months before.

Opposite *Jubilant Sandinista forces, after the overthrow of Anastasio Somoza, who had fled the country, celebrate through the streets of Managua, Nicaragua's capital.*

'It was eleven in the morning. The planes full of National Guards were taking off one by one. The radio kept repeating that the Guards were laying down their guns, that they were leaving. I could feel it everywhere – victory. But I was still

8

9

Right *Anastasio Somoza, who fled Nicaragua as Sandinista forces closed on Managua on 17 July 1979, had become one of the richest persons in Central America in one of the poorest countries.*

waiting for my boys to come home. Many others had already shown up. It was eleven o'clock, and I hadn't even made the coffee or breakfast or anything.

'Then some kids came in shouting, "Doña Maria! Henry's coming!" I hadn't seen or heard from him for days and days, and there he was, marching down the other side of the street. I was crazy with happiness, blowing him kisses in the air. Half an hour later Javier, the second one, turned up riding a jeep painted FREE COUNTRY OR DEATH. I cried out to him too.

'But there was still one missing – my youngest. I went inside, wringing my hands and thinking, "My baby's missing! They've killed my little boy!" Everyone from the neighbourhood had appeared, all but my little one. I went outside again and watched and waited. Someone said they saw Enrique coming, riding a tank, others said no, it wasn't him. I was afraid it wasn't the truth. Then suddenly I saw him. He was coming. I ran over, held him, touched him, embraced him. It seemed impossible that he had come!' (Maria Cano, Managuan housewife.)

Other parents were not able to welcome back their children. More than 10,000 had died in the war against Somoza in the preceding seven weeks of the FSLN's final offensive. Somoza's National Guard had responded by attacking the Nicaraguan people with unbelievable ferocity.

'In Leon that day, people were running along the street, screaming, "The Guard's going to burn down the whole neighbourhood – everybody out! They're going to start shelling!" Then the Guard turned up and started shooting through the doors, shouting and trying to smash them down.

'All my neighbours ran out, mothers with their kids in their arms, old people stumbling along. We didn't know what to do or where to go. We were afraid of crossing the railroad tracks because on the other side, in the bushes of the empty lots, there was a whole army with tanks and tractors.

'Suddenly, some Guards came out of the bushes and stopped us. They lined up a group of about 25 men, young and old, made them lie on the ground, and searched them. Then they told them to kneel down. And then just one Guard machine-gunned them down.

'In my street alone, 22 people of all ages were killed. They were humble and peaceful people.' (Anonymous evidence given to the Inter-American Commission on Human Rights, November 1978.)

But such brutality only helped to swell the ranks of the FSLN:

'Whenever we took a town, the whole population came out to watch. Then we called for new recruits ... We never lacked people. Only arms.' (Omar Cabezas, FSLN Commander.)

'It was like putting on the final reel of a war movie. A violent and bloody end seemed inevitable to everyone. And we all accepted it as our immediate fate. No one was prepared to say "no" to violence if the alternative was the perpetuation of Somoza.' (Managuan lawyer, 1979.)

Below *The portrait of Augusto Cesar Sandino, next to the red and black flag of the Sandinista Front for National Liberation, is held aloft to celebrate the success of the Sandinistas over Somoza and his National Guard. The father of Anastasio Somoza, who bore the same name, was responsible for the assassination of Sandino in 1934.*

On 17 July 1979, Anastasio Somoza fled Nicaragua for the United States where he was admitted on a tourist and business visa, valid for four years. He owned extensive properties in Florida and had hoarded away considerable riches in Miami banks. He was to live there for one year before being assassinated in Paraguay in a brutal and sordid way.

With the flight of Somoza a provisional *junta*, made up of

members of the FSLN, the Church, and business representatives, was established to govern the country until elections. The *junta* flew to Nicaragua from Costa Rica where they had been in exile, to establish a temporary capital in Leon, the country's second largest city. The Sandinistas' victory over Somoza came suddenly, and almost peacefully, with his flight into exile.

Left *Victorious Sandinista forces and Managuans in front of the National Palace, July 1979.*

Right *Cuban leader, Fidel Castro, addressing crowds during his triumphal drive towards Havana, 6 January 1959.*

Below *The close proximity of 'communist' Cuba to the USA has been a cause for concern to the US government for many years.*

2
Nicaragua

Since 1959 the Cuban revolution and Cuban leader Fidel Castro have represented a threat to the interests of the US government in Central America. Cuba's attempts to 'export' revolution in the 1960s only served to reinforce this concern. Relations between the two countries were broken off in 1961, although by 1963, President Kennedy was looking for ways to restore communication. US fears of Cuba resulted in the failed Bay of Pigs invasion of 1961 and, in 1962, almost brought the world to war over the Cuban Missile Crisis. Attempts to re-establish relations in the 1970s came to nothing, largely due to the antagonism of Zbigniew Bzreszinski, the US National Security Adviser, who was opposed to any 'deal' with Cuba. The election of Ronald Reagan in 1980, who favoured a hard line against Cuba and the Soviet Union, effectively put an end to improving relations.

In 1981 the US Ambassador to the United Nations, Jeanne Kirkpatrick, declared that the Soviet-Cuban communist 'menace' in Central America made it 'the most important place in the world for the United States today'. Ronald Reagan, in both his statements and actions on many occasions appears to have agreed with her. The analysis in 1980 by Ambler Moss, the US Ambassador to Panama, was perhaps more prudent: 'What we see in Central America today would not be much different if Fidel Castro and the Soviet Union did not exist.' Nowhere is this statement more relevant than in the case of Nicaragua.

Nicaragua became independent from Spain, which had controlled the New World for 300 years, in a number of stages which contributed to her later instability. Firstly, she became part of the Mexican Empire in 1822, then part of the Central American Federation in 1823. Finally, in 1838 Nicaragua became an independent state.

US interest in Nicaragua grew in the nineteenth century as the United States moved its frontiers westwards and became a Pacific, as well as an Atlantic, power. A route was

Managua
Granada
Lake
Nicaragua
R. San Juan
COSTA RICA
Pacific Ocean
NICARAGUA
Leon
Matagalpa
R. Tuma
R. Coco
HONDURAS
Mosquito Coast
Caribbean
Sea
0   100   200 Km

MEXICO
BELIZE
HONDURAS
Caribbean Sea
GUATEMALA
NICARAGUA
EL SALVADOR
PANAMA
COSTA RICA
Pacific Ocean

Above *A map of Nicaragua, showing its important position in the middle of Central America, with an extensive coastline on to the Caribbean.*

needed to link the two oceans. The San Juan River, next to Costa Rica, led conveniently from the Atlantic coast into Lake Nicaragua, leaving just 19 km of land to cross to reach the Pacific. The Californian gold rush encouraged renewed interest in Nicaragua.

US involvement in Central America led to rivalry with Britain which had long been established in the region. The underlying cause of the rivalry was the growing political, economic and military strength of the United States, and its determination to halt Britain's advance in the region. The Clayton-Bulwer Treaty of 1850, in which the United States and Britain agreed, among other things, not to colonize Central America, did not contribute to peace in Nicaragua nor end the rivalry. Rather, Britain and the United States contributed to the strife already present there by supporting rival political factions. The British supported the Conservatives. The Liberals, based in the city of Leon, gained the help of an American named William Walker. Walker was an adventurer who sailed to Nicaragua with other mercenaries in 1855 to obtain whatever advantage he could from the country. After taking the city of Granada, Walker set himself up as 'President' of Nicaragua, a 'presidency' soon recognised by the President of the United States. However, as the nineteenth century came to a close, the US need for an oceanic link for economic and military purposes became more pressing. Nicaragua was passed over as the site of the route, as the United States engineered events in Panama so as to gain control over a canal there. When Britain and Japan were discovered discussing the building of a rival canal with President Zelaya of Nicaragua, US pressures led to an uprising which toppled the President.

Below *The building of the Panama Canal gave the United States considerable influence in the Panama Canal Zone and in the region as a whole.*

The US invades

The governments which followed did little for Nicaragua's development or stability and the United States found reason to intervene on occasion by sending in the US Marines. They were concerned that a stable and friendly government (friendly to the United States, that is) be established in Nicaragua, since it occupied a position in the middle of Central America, as well as reaching to the Caribbean Sea. Both these areas were, as they still are, considered the United States' 'backyard'. The first time the US Marines invaded Nicaragua was to put down a rebellion led by Benjamin Zeledon in 1912. They remained on Nicaraguan soil until they were recalled in 1925.

The second invasion of Nicaragua was in 1926, when the country was again in civil war, and the Marines remained until 1933. This invasion was to prove more crucial than anyone could have realized. The rise of the Somoza family and the police force, the National Guard, was engineered by the United States in 1927, and it became a double-headed monster which soon took on awesome proportions. The National Guard was designed by the United States to maintain order and it provided not only the means by which the Somoza dynasty could begin its dictatorship over Nicaragua, but also a focus of discontent.

The US invasion had its opponents. Rebel leader Augusto Cesar Sandino's resistance to the occupation was to be the model for the struggle in the 1960s. Sandino was killed in 1934, lured to his death by the National Guard to be shot down in cold blood. Although the revolutionary movement which he had led in the countryside, and which had inflicted the first defeat on occupying US forces anywhere in the world, died with him, his ideas lived on. They were to be rekindled in the 1960s by the Sandinista Front for National Liberation (FSLN), who took their name from Sandino.

Anastasio Somoza Garcia took power in 1936, retaining it with the support of both the National Guard, whose leadership he encouraged to be as corrupt as he was himself, and the United States, which turned a blind eye to his brutality and repression in return for obedient support. Anastasio Somoza was assassinated in 1956 to be succeeded by his son Luis Somoza Debayle. This Somoza was softer in approach than his father but left no doubts that Nicaragua was still firmly under the same management. Another Somoza, Anastasio Somoza Debayle, (younger brother to Luis),

Opposite *The earthquake, which flattened a large part of Managua in 1972, profited Somoza and favoured members of his National Guard, who openly stole money given as aid to Nicaragua.*

became President in 1967 in a now-familiar corrupt election. Not only did he share his father's name but his taste for harsher forms of control as well.

Somoza's downfall

The fortunes of the FSLN, which had suffered crippling defeats in the 1960s, improved in the 1970s. The 1972 earthquake, which killed 10,000 people and razed to the ground a large part of Managua, showed Somoza at his most despicable. Millions of dollars of relief funds, which had flowed into Nicaragua from a world appalled by the scale of the tragedy, were corruptly siphoned off by Somoza himself and shared with highly favoured members of the National Guard. Opposition to Somoza in the form of strikes and demonstrations became more common, despite the brutality of the National Guard in putting them down. The Catholic

Below *In Jinotepe, a masked member of the Sandinistas stands defiantly next to the slogan, 'there is no human or technical force capable of holding us back.'*

Church in Nicaragua, which until then had ignored the Somozas' excesses, also began to speak out. The FSLN began to attract young women and men to their ranks from throughout the whole of society.

As the 1970s came to a close, Somoza, protected from the realities of the world around him by the 'Bunker' of his reinforced military headquarters, was under attack from outside as well as inside his country. The US President, Jimmy Carter, was applying pressure to Somoza to make reparation for the worst human rights record in all Latin America. The press inside Nicaragua, silent for too long, began to report criminal acts perpetrated by Somoza and the National Guards. Pedro Chamorro, whose newspapers attacked Somoza, was killed by the National Guard on his

Above *This student, killed by the National Guard in Nicaragua, was one of many women who fought for the FSLN against Somoza.*

21

Right *Eden Pastora, who was known as 'Commander Zero' whilst a member of the FSLN, leaving Managua after a daring attack which freed a number of Sandinista prisoners and boosted the morale of all those opposed to Somoza. Pastora later rejected the Sandinista cause to become a 'Contra'.*

way to work. His death caused a further surge of resistance to Somoza. The FSLN grew in strength and audacity. In August 1978, 25 members of the FSLN, led by 'Commander Zero', Eden Pastora (later to join the *Contras*), took over the National Palace in Managua, posing as National Guards, and held 1,500 people to ransom. Somoza was forced to concede to their demands. Following the example of the FSLN, ordinary people began to take control of their own lives and defy the National Guard.

In June 1978, the FSLN, now united in a more efficient organization, launched their final offensive against Somoza with the help of more effective weapons captured from the enemy and supplied from outside sources. When, on 17 July, Somoza fled to Miami, victory was at hand for the FSLN. Two days later they entered Managua.

3
The United States and the Sandinista revolution

The legacy of Somoza to Nicaragua was more than just a memory of nearly half a century of misrule by his family. Over 50,000 people had been killed in the war, 100,000 had been wounded, and 40,000 war orphans created. A fifth of the population was homeless, a third of the workforce unemployed. Coffee and cotton crops, essential to the economy, had either not been planted or had rotted in the fields through lack of care. Huge loans from foreign banks had been salted away by Somoza leaving Nicaragua with a US $1.6 billion debt, the highest per capita in the whole of Latin America. The damage to the economy caused by the war was calculated at US $18 million, some of it deliberately caused by Somoza who, in a last-minute act of vengeance, ordered his airforce to bomb factories and farms to add to the already massive problems of reconstruction facing the new government of the Sandinistas.

The new government, called the Government of National Reconstruction in an effort to gain the commitment of everyone to the rebuilding of Nicaragua, was made up of a majority of FSLN members together with representatives of other political parties, business, and the Church. The government's aim was to rebuild the shattered economy and unite society. This was to prove a formidable task, and with the external pressures which developed, the task became herculean. Housing, education, health and welfare, which were far from priorities under Somoza, now became so, rather than the creation of individual wealth.

The FSLN emerged from the struggle against Somoza as the most important political force in Nicaragua. It generated

Above *Reservists of the Sandinista army take a break after fighting 'Contras' on the Nicaraguan/ Honduran border.*

a range of organizations which effectively covered the political activities of the country. This caused great suspicion, even alarm, in Washington where the US government feared 'another Cuba' was being set up.

Despite this degree of control, however, the Sandinistas professed not to seek a totalitarian State. In the economy the private sector maintained its position. The full range of political parties continued to exist (not all of them sympathetic to the aims and policies of the Sandinistas), as did a press which reflected their interests. Nor was vengeance sought against the National Guard despite the fact that many commanders of the FSLN had been cruelly tortured in their hands. Perhaps reflecting the Christian influence in the revolution, the death penalty was abolished. Many thousands of National Guards were released after their trials in People's Courts. However, the decision was made to put off elections until some of the essential work of reconstruction had been completed.

A cold wind from the north

The FSLN sought friendly, mutually-respectful, relations with the United States. Nicaragua, a tiny country in comparison, hardly represented a military threat to that great nation. Yet, the Sandinistas had no wish to be dominated and controlled by the US as had been the case under Somoza. However, from the start of 'the beautiful revolution', which is how Nicaraguans described events after 1979, the United States has been not only suspicious but antagonistic. As a last act of his presidency Jimmy Carter resumed supplies of arms to Somoza to keep out the Sandinistas. A change of President in 1980 saw the US position become even more hostile: Ronald Reagan's government represented a new cold wind from the north. Nicaragua was identified with Cuba, the Soviet Union and the advance of communism, which had to be halted by any means and at whatever cost. US aid to Nicaragua was suspended, and credits to buy essential foodstuffs withdrawn. The US government began to lobby Western governments to isolate Nicaragua, in much the same way as Cuba was isolated from the rest of the world after 1961.

US hostility was not just economic and political, although that was damaging enough. National Guards, who had fled to other countries in Central America and to the United States in 1979, received support and training from the US Central Intelligence Agency (CIA) and other agencies, and began to launch attacks from across Nicaragua's borders with Honduras and Costa Rica. The attacks were wanton criminal attacks, usually on poor peasants and workers trying to support themselves and build their lives after the war.

The *Contras*, as they became known throughout the world (from *contra-revolucionarios*, counter revolutionaries), also attacked teachers involved in the Literacy Campaign, and people from other countries who had gone to assist Nicaragua in its task of rebuilding. The *Contras*, who were corrupt and brutal under Somoza, were no less so in their new guise. Many acted like bandits, robbing, murdering and raping.

The support given to the *Contras* by the US government has been colossal; in 1981 President Reagan authorized US$19 million, by 1986 this figure had risen to US$100 million. Nor do these official sums include the full amounts given to the *Contras* from private (and other public) US sources.

A suffering economy

Nearly half of the Nicaraguan budget since 1979 has been diverted to defence to deal with the threat posed by the *Contras* which has resulted in a shortage of capital for investment in reconstruction, in the economy, and in the social structure. Hence shortages in all areas have resulted. Stores lack day-to-day articles such as soap and toothpaste, petrol is in chronic short supply, schools try to function without pencils and paper, hospitals without so much as an Aspirin or bandages. Such shortages and frustrations, together with the deaths of loved ones in the border fighting with the *Contras* have contributed to the decline in popularity of the Sandinistas since 1979.

The Sandinistas' policies have sometimes contributed to that unpopularity as well. The over-zealous relocation of the Miskito, and other Indian people, on the Atlantic coast in 1982, drove them into the arms of the *Contras* as well as losing friends to the Sandinistas' cause throughout the world. The closing down of the opposition paper, *La Prensa*, achieved the same result. Sandinista economic policies, which antagonized peasant farmers, resulted in shortages of basic agricultural produce in the market-place. Continual 'States of Emergency' since 1982, resulting in the curtailment of some human rights, have aroused great concern among many sympathetic to the Sandinistas. However, the Sandinistas have acknowledged their early mistakes with the Miskitos and have worked hard and with considerable success to remedy them. A policy of autonomy for the Atlantic coast has persuaded many to stop fighting.

The only 'success' of the *Contras* is in diverting resources to defence, away from areas like the economy and social services, which would improve the standard of living of the people and, thereby, the popularity of the Sandinistas. However, as long as the US government remains committed to the destruction of the government in Managua, support of the *Contras* is the only option open to it at present, short of an all-out invasion.

Some effective attempts by the United States at sabotage against Nicaragua, have occurred. In 1984 Nicaraguan ports were mined by CIA agents in order to keep out supplies, thought to be arms, from the Soviet Union. In 1987, Colonel Oliver North and Admiral John Poindexter gave evidence to a special US Senate Committee of the way in which the profits derived from arms sold to the regime of

Opposite *Eden Pastora supervising the unloading of supplies from the US government for his 'Contras'. They were never enough for Pastora, who retired from the fight against the Sandinistas in 1986.*

27

Above *CIA agent, Eugene Hasenfus, being led away by a Sandinista soldier after parachuting from his plane, which had been shot down while dropping supplies to 'Contras' inside Nicaragua.*

Opposite *'A VOTE FOR THE FATHERLAND'. Sandinistas waiting to vote in the country's elections in 1984.*

the Ayatollah Khomeini in Iran (an 'enemy' of the United States since the seizure of embassy officials in Teheran in 1980) were diverted to the *Contras*. In the summer of 1987 President Reagan was preparing the ground to demand more funds for the *Contras* from the US Congress.

In an attempt to deflect US attacks, both political and military, and to maintain support among friendly Western nations, the Sandinistas have made conciliatory gestures towards the United States. In response to US claims of a massive build up of Cuban troops in Nicaragua, a much-publicized return home of Cuban military advisers occurred in 1985, along with Cuban teachers and workers. In November 1984 elections were held, partly in response to US claims of a drift towards totalitarianism. These were the first elections in revolutionary Nicaragua and, probably, the most open and honest in the country's history. Certainly, foreign

29

Right *Daniel Ortega, Nicaragua's President and leading member of the FSLN, denounces the policies of the United States government against his country, which force Nicaragua to spend half its budget on defence.*

observers, invited to ensure the proper running and fairness of the elections, were impressed. A total of 82% of Nicaraguans turned out to vote. The FSLN took nearly 70% of the vote.

The elected President, Daniel Ortega, offered an amnesty to the *Contras* at the first meeting of the National Assembly in January 1985. However, this offer met neither a favourable response from the *Contras* nor from the US government. Nothing the Sandinistas could do seemed able to deflect the US Administration from its determination to destroy them by force.

Not surprisingly, when Daniel Ortega spoke at the United Nations General Assembly in July 1986 he referred to the US government's 'state terrorism' against Nicaragua. He spoke of the 31,000 Nicaraguans, out of a population of 2.5 million, who had already 'fallen victim to this dirty war, this cruel war imposed upon us.' The US UN Representative, General Vernon Walters, denounced Ortega's speech. The US government was no less dismissive of the International Court's ruling that the US policy against Nicaragua was illegal, should cease, and that compensation should be paid for past acts. In spite of this, and the later revelations of the 'Irangate' hearing, the United States remained unshakable in its support for the *Contras*.

4
El Salvador: terror by death squads

World attention became focused upon El Salvador, the smallest country in Central America, in the late 1970s, when a number of priests were murdered and others tortured, by government forces. The existence of so-called, 'death squads', which emerged from among right-wing groups in the army and police, horrified the world. A leaflet distributed by one death squad urged, 'BE A PATRIOT, KILL A PRIEST'. The most prominent priest to be killed was Archbishop Oscar Romero. Since becoming Archbishop in 1977

Below *El Salvador is on the Pacific coast of Central America. Honduras and Guatemala are its immediate neighbours.*

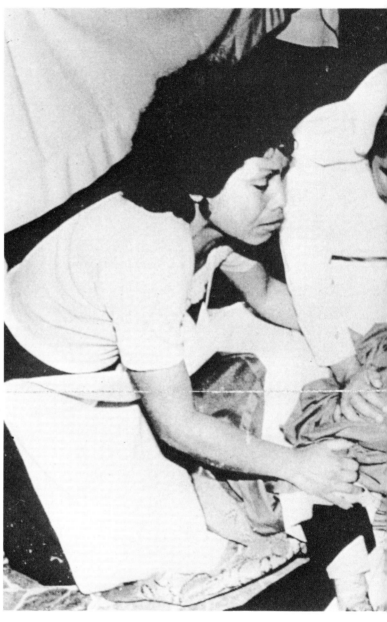

Archbishop Oscar Romero, assassinated whilst saying mass. Archbishop Romero had spoken out against the government and for the people suffering in El Salvador's civil war.

he had spoken out against the kidnappings and murders that were occurring almost daily in his country, demanding that the government release victims, or provide information about them. He spoke as well, of social justice and of the right of the people to oppose oppression. In March 1980 he

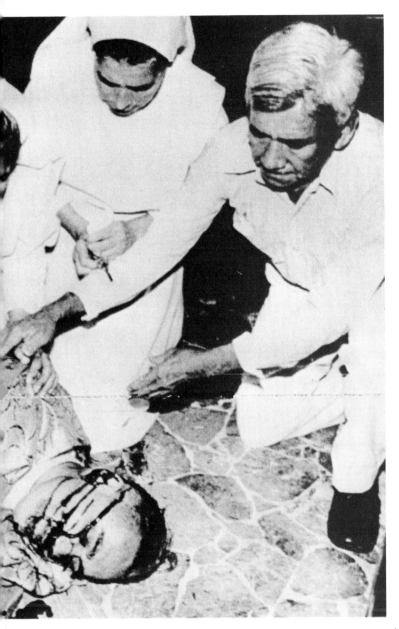

was shot by an assassin in front of his congregation while
holding mass in the Chapel of the Divine Providence Cancer
Hospital where he lived. Shortly before, Romero had made
an appeal to President Carter urging him not to send in any
more arms.

A poverty-stricken country

El Salvador is a highly overpopulated country with few opportunities for country people to obtain their own land. The proportion of landless peasants has risen from 12% of the rural population in the 1960s, to over 65% in the 1980s. By contrast, 2% of the population, about 200 families, own 60% of the land and receive a third of the country's income. These families, the oligarchy, control the most important sectors of the economy from which great political power has traditionally flowed. Once consisting of just fourteen families, the oligarchy has historically maintained its position in society through force, and in more recent times through the army and the police.

In the 1960s, new political parties and trade unions came into existence, putting their faith in change in electoral politics. At the same time the United States encouraged the build-up of the Salvadorean army and the security forces. However, corruption and fraud (such as that seen in the 1972 elections when the victorious coalition of parties was kept out of office) diverted disillusioned Salvadoreans into the politics of direct action. Guerrilla organizations began to form, but the most phenomenal development was the explosion of 'popular' political organizations. Thousands of people joined these organizations and peacefully occupied land on behalf of peasant farmers, and the public buildings and factories of the cities. When these organizations joined forces with the guerrillas they combined military struggle and political activity, representing a formidable and radical force for change and a threat to the existing order. The Church too, became increasingly involved in the demand for social change. Indeed many of the organizations resulted from the consciousness-raising activities of the Church. In the 1970s, El Salvador's bishops issued protests at the violation of human rights and at the injustices which characterized their society. Archbishop Romero became a well-known and outspoken critic of the government and a champion of civil rights and social justice.

In response to the challenge presented by the growth of opposition groups, and the Church's increasingly active role in society, right wing death squads began to assassinate priests, peasants, students and trade unionists; in fact, anyone who was perceived as representing a threat to established interests. The death toll mounted rapidly and El Salvador became locked in bloody civil war.

Opposite *Growing up in El Salvador. These children are refugees from the bombings and massacres in El Salvador's civil war in the 1980s.*

US involvement

The United States, whose interest in El Salvador was strategic rather than economic, became closely involved in political events there in 1961 through their support for a counter-coup which overthrew the young officers who had taken power the year before. From then on, out of fear of 'communist expansion in the region', the United States encouraged the build-up of the Salvadorean Army and the Security Forces.

Repression at the hands of government forces became a daily reality for Salvadoreans. The United States was very active again in 1972 after that year's fraudulent elections. US intervention put down a coup which would have reintroduced constitutional rule to El Salvador. This interference brought about the imposition of a president, Colonel Molina, who acted harshly towards all forms of opposition. The role of the United States during the 1970s served to strengthen the hand of the military and effectively undermine moderate political groups. Salvadorean politics became increasingly polarised. With other forms of political action cut off, the numbers in guerrilla groups grew. As the 1970s came to a close the established order in El Salvador was maintained only through the political violence of the army and the security forces. The Church became one of the main targets. A Catholic University was bombed, priests were expelled, others tortured and killed. The government of Jimmy Carter emphasized the importance of human rights. The human rights record of El Salvador was so appalling that it caused the United States government to suspend a US $90 million loan, albeit temporarily.

By the beginning of the 1980s. El Salvador appeared on the brink of a complete upheaval; the government was threatened with a coup from the right and an insurrection from the left. The US government, faced with the Sandinista revolution in Nicaragua, was under great pressure to develop a policy for El Salvador which would result in stability there.

When Ronald Reagan became President of the United States in 1981, he saw evidence of 'communist interference in El Salvador', which he intended to halt. He poured military aid into the region to bring about 'stability'. The killings continued; 7,700 in the first four months of 1981, most of them linked to government security forces. Tens of thousands of trade unionists, teachers, peasants, and

Opposite *Roberto D'Aubuisson, leader of the right-wing Arena party, was banned from entering the United States in the 1980s because of evidence linking him with atrocities in El Salvador.*

36

students had 'disappeared' in El Salvador in addition to those known to have been killed. The US government's support in the 1980s was given to Jose Napoleon Duarte, leader of the Christian Democrat Party. Duarte, with US political and material assistance, enjoyed considerable electoral successes in 1984 and 1985 and, aided by infighting among the right wing forces, and the failure of the guerrilla movement to make headway, was able to consolidate his position. Nevertheless, the FMLN guerrillas still controlled more than a third of the country and were capable of spectacular successes against the army.

Right *José Napoleon Duarte was elected president of El Salvador in 1984.*

In February 1984, Duarte's government met with the guerrillas, raising hopes of a ceasefire. Further talks in 1985 led nowhere and hostilities resumed, resulting in a stalemate for both sides. While the war continues, eating up 40% of El Salvador's budget, Duarte, or his successor will remain unable to implement the rise in living standards which could deprive the FMLN/FDR coalition of support. The guerrillas know they cannot be militarily defeated, that they are a force to be reckoned with, and that one day they will have a say in the running of their country.

Above *All the weapons and equipment of the National Guard in El Salvador were provided by the United States government who played a very influential role there.*

5

Sucked into the quagmire: Honduras and Costa Rica

Below *The proximity of Honduras and Costa Rica to Nicaragua has involved them in that country's problems.*

Both Honduras and Costa Rica became caught up in the Central American crisis for no other reason than their geographical position as neighbours to Nicaragua.

Historically, Honduras has been intimately linked to US policy and actions in Central America. In 1954 Honduras was the staging post for the CIA-organized coup which

toppled the elected government of Jacobo Arbenz in Guatemala. In 1961, Swan Island, off the Honduran Atlantic coast, was the communications centre for the CIA-sponsored invasion of Cuba. In 1965 Honduras contributed greatly to the US invasion of the Dominican Republic. Yet despite this, for a long time during the 1980s, the Honduran Government denied the existence of the 20,000 armed *Contras*, who operated out of Honduras for their attacks into Nicaragua. In the period 1985–87 there were more than twenty Nicaraguan incursions into Honduras to destroy *Contra* camps. In March 1986, when such an attack occurred, the Honduran army refused to admit the incident until forced to do so by the US government, which threatened to cut off US $20 million in aid unless they did. Only when Honduran forces were dispatched to the area was the aid forthcoming, together with US $60 million more military aid.

Honduras is important to the United States government as a 'front line' state in the US war against the Sandinistas in Nicaragua and the FMLN in El Salvador. Not only does the United States liberally support the *Contras* on Honduran soil, but also conducts large-scale manoeuvres there, like the 'Cabanas '86' exercises which involved 7,000 US troops. Permanent barracks, airstrips, and radar installations, (all of which are illegal under US law) have been built in Honduras. Many observers, and the Sandinistas themselves, consider these to be preparations for a full-scale invasion of Nicaragua. In return for these services the United States provides Honduras with military and economic aid which gives the US government enormous political leverage over Honduras. Aid can be withheld to assure compliance. Honduras risks becoming little more than a military outpost of the United States in Central America.

Costa Rica

Costa Rica, which is known as the only Central American state without an army, has also become caught up in the region's turmoil despite attempts by successive presidents to remain 'neutral'. A number of *Contra* groups have conducted raids into Nicaragua, operating from Costa Rica and the United States has used the country as a secret base for training the *Contras*. The *Contras* in Costa Rica, as in Honduras, present not only a political problem to their unwilling host but have also been shown to be involved in drug

43

In Costa Rica the Guardia Civil attempt to control the activities of 'Contras' operating on their border with Nicaragua. The US CIA operated secret airfields in Costa Rica for the benefit of the 'Contras' unknown to the country's government.

Right *Despite the embrace between the presidents of the United States (Ronald Reagan) and Honduras (Roberto Cordova), Honduran people, and their government were unhappy at being sucked into the unrest spreading across Central America.*

trafficking, and to act like bandits. Costa Rica can no longer claim not to possess a military force; circumstances have dictated otherwise. Since 1981 the government has been forced to allocate an increasing proportion of its budget to security. The Civil and Rural Guard have increased in number. Until 1985 they were outgunned and outmanned by the *Contras*. The United States gave US $2.7 million in military aid, and US and Israeli military advisers have trained counter-insurgency forces. The Costa Rican government was considerably embarrassed, however, by evidence at the 'Irangate' Senate hearings which showed that the US government had built a secret airstrip in their country without their knowledge or permission.

It looked as if both these countries were being inexorably dragged down into a conflict of increasingly region-wide proportions. Fear of this outcome spurred President Oscar Arias of Costa Rica to present a new peace proposal which, to many people's surprise was signed by all five Central American presidents at Esquipulas, Guatemala on 7th August 1987. For this initiative (often called the Arias plan) Arias was awarded the Nobel Peace Prize. History will show whether this marked a turning point in Central America.

6
Guatemala

Jacobo Arbenz Guzman was elected President of Guatemala in 1951, having gained almost twice as many votes as the other candidates combined. Arbenz was interested in land reform since the ownership of land was a major political, as well as social, problem in Guatemala. About 2% of the population owned 70% of the land. The largest land owner was United Fruit, an American organization, which held considerable areas of uncultivated land. In March 1953 Arbenz expropriated 95 uncultivated hectares (234,000 acres) of land from United Fruit, offering them compensation in return.

As well as demanding a much more favourable compensation package, United Fruit, making full use of the US media,

Below *Instability in Guatemala and Belize is pushing both countries towards involvement in the crisis enveloping the rest of Central America.*

also responded by launching a campaign emphasizing the positive aspects of its relationship with Guatemala. The most dramatic point it wished to make in its campaign, however, was that Guatemala was at risk from communism. Whipped up by the campaign, anti-communism reached hysterical proportions in Guatemala and the United States, and in 1953 President Eisenhower agreed to a CIA plan to remove Arbenz.

There was little Arbenz could do to prevent this inevitable course of action. In June 1954, he was overthrown and replaced by Colonel Castillo Armas, who had been hand-picked by the CIA to lead the attack. Meanwhile, United Fruit received back their expropriated land and a windfall of US$11 million when taxes on foreign investors were abolished.

Below *The five-man junta which overthrew Arbenz and took office in 1954. Their leader, Colonel Castillo Armas is second left.*

US influence, along with that of the army, remained very strong in Guatemala. By the 1980s the US government was extremely concerned about the situation there. Apart from Mexico, Guatemala possessed the most experienced guerrilla movement in Central America which had grown considerably since the 1950s.

Army repression of Guatemalan Indians, who make up 60% of the country's population, had resulted in a move

Above *US President Eisenhower in 1954. A year earlier he had given his blessing to the CIA plan to replace Arbenz in Guatemala.*

49

towards radical politics. As in El Salvador, right wing death squads had been formed to attack anyone perceived as belonging to the opposition. During 1981 death squad killings were reported to be 35–40 people a day. Most victims, invariably Indian people, showed signs of torture. As many as 100,000 people have been killed or have 'disappeared' in Guatemala since the army took over from Arbenz in 1954.

Large numbers of Indians were massacred by government forces simply because they belonged to villages suspected of being sympathetic to the guerrillas. The massacres resulted in even more guerrilla recruits coming from among the Indians. Whole Indian communities have been deliberately uprooted, separated from one another, and put under the control of the military. Similar tactics were used, without any success, during the American war against Vietnam. As many as half a million have fled as refugees into Mexico.

Large-scale US aid to Guatemala was resumed in 1985–86. At US $90 million the amount was small by comparison with other Central American countries, but represented an advance to Guatemala whose aid had been stopped six years before because of its human rights record. Guatemala's human rights record was no better in 1985, but the US government was prepared to turn a blind eye because it now had an elected civilian president and could

Below *Guatemalan Indian people have suffered greatest in the attacks the government has made against those identified as a danger to its survival.*

technically be called a 'democracy'. Changes of government since 1954 appear to have made little difference to the political, economic and social scene in Guatemala, a country which seems poised, as it has for decades, for a complete social upheaval of unprecedented scale even by Central American standards.

Above In Guatemala, senior Army officers put themselves on display after the overthrow of President Rios Montt in 1984.

Belize

Once described as a 'haven of peace in a war-torn Central America' even Belize, Guatemala's neighbour, and the last British outpost in Central America, has not been able to fully escape the crisis in the region.

The Belizean economy is becoming increasingly dependent upon the US market or US-owned companies (in 1985 a consortium headed by Coca-Cola Foods bought land comprising one eighth the area of the country in order to develop citrus production) and Belize is finding itself increasingly under US political pressures which it may well not be able to ignore. Historical issues, such as the unresolved problem of Belize's border with Guatemala, continue to loom. Honduras and Mexico, Belize's other neighbours, also have long-standing territorial claims.

The presence of British troops and jump-jets, effectively maintains a status-quo between Belize and Guatemala, and has also served to keep Belize out of a deeper involvement in Central American problems. There is pressure from Washington and within Belize itself, to replace the British troops with a US force. Should this happen, the likelihood of Belize sliding towards greater involvement in the crisis is undoubted. In 1985, Belize resisted pressure to accept

British troops patrol the borders between Belize and Guatemala since a dispute over territory has threatened to escalate into outright conflict.

military aid from the United States but agreed a compromise. The US now provides non-military aid and US military advisers have joined their British counterparts in the Belizean defence force. However, it is unlikely to be long before Belize's economic dependence on the United States forces her to bend to further pressure.

7
The shark and the sardines

The United States and Central America

By the mid 1980s the spectre of Vietnam was haunting the United States, and the rest of the world. Fears were being expressed that US policies would lead to another 'Vietnam' in Central America. The build-up of aid, military supplies, military advisers, and political involvement with repressive regimes in Central America appeared to resemble too closely the US involvement in Southeast Asia in the 1960s. Despite the misgivings of a significant proportion of the population, the United States has become the principal actor in the Central American crisis.

The United States became interested in Central America long before President Reagan authorized support for the *Contras*, or 'Freedom Fighters' as he prefers to call them. Theodore Roosevelt had already formulated US policy which was to remain until the 1980s; since revolutions caused disorder and instability the United States would act as policeman in the region to ensure they did not occur.

US policies were severely put to the test in Nicaragua from 1927–33. Sandino showed, as has been demonstrated throughout Central America ever since, that a guerrilla force could survive ground and air attacks even from the most powerful nation in the world. The United States had to devise another way of dealing with Sandino. They organized a national police force, in this case the National Guard, who could ensure stability without the necessity to 'send in the Marines'. Unfortunately for Central American nations they had no say in the matter and, regrettably, this kind of stability encouraged repression and obstructed reform.

US economic power also conferred control. US economic might was so great, and Central American economies so

Opposite *This cartoon makes a wry comment about the US/Nicaragua involvement.*

54

The Cuban revolution in 1959 inspired others in the region to follow Cuba's example. In Nicaragua in 1960 an effigy of the US Ambassador is hanged, and the 'Stars and Stripes' trampled upon, in an anti-US demonstration.

dependent upon US markets and supplies, that economic links could be used to maintain US interests and Central American stability. Thus, US military might was avoided and the image of the 'good neighbour', as US foreign policy in the region was called after 1933, could be maintained. By the 1950s economic problems loosened the ties which bound the region. In Cuba, Fidel Castro seized power greatly alarming the United States; if socialism could win in Cuba, why not elsewhere?

In the 1960s President Kennedy introduced the Alliance for Progress as the last chance to resolve the region's problems through peaceful means, warning, at the same time, that those who made peaceful revolutions impossible would make violent ones inevitable. The aim of the Alliance was to

Below

President Kennedy, photographed in 1963. He introduced the Alliance for Progress plan, hoping it would help solve the problems in Central America.

use some of the immense wealth of the United States to develop the economies of the whole of Latin America and thereby encourage the formation and development of a strong middle class which would set the pace for democratic change. However, the elites and the military in El Salvador, Nicaragua, Guatemala, and Honduras used the new wealth for themselves. The reforms, in housing, in health, in education and in social provision, which were to accompany the Alliance's injection of capital, did not occur. Inevitably, just as President Kennedy had forecast, revolutionary movements began to spring up; in Nicaragua, in Guatemala, and in El Salvador. The Alliance for Progress had failed.

Whilst President Nixon in the late 1960s and early 1970s attempted to control regimes in Central America through arms sales, President Carter in 1976 turned to human rights. He was to be no more successful than Nixon. The ambiguity

Above *Henry Kissinger is greeted by the Honduran Foreign Minister in 1983. He was on a fact-finding tour of the region as president of the US Commission on Central America.*

59

Above *Protestors demonstrating against US policy in Central America, February 1987.*

of his position resulted in giving arms to Somoza in Nicaragua to combat the Sandinistas and, at the same time, attempting to curb human rights abuses committed by the National Guard in Somoza's name. Ronald Reagan, who succeeded Carter as US President, had an altogether simpler vision. Since authoritarian regimes, like Somoza's in Nicaragua, were friendly to the United States it was in its interest to support such regimes, whether they honoured human rights or not.

President Reagan's policies confer, at best, short-term stability by disguising the deep-rooted structural problems of economies and societies in Central America. Unless the problems are confronted, the result, for Central America, will be a slide towards social upheaval and revolution.

8
Central America and the world

On 3 December 1980, St Mathew's Cathedral, Washington D.C., was filled with worshippers who had gathered to pray for peace in Central America. The occasion coincided with the funeral in San Salvador of the leaders of the Democratic Revolutionary Front (FDR) who had been killed the week before. Just before the mass, word came that four American missionaries were missing. Jean Donovan, Maura Clarke, Ita Ford, and Dorothy Kazel were discovered shortly afterwards. They had been murdered and their bodies buried. Their deaths, like that of Archbishop Romero who had been assassinated in San Salvador the previous March, caused outrage throughout the world and a heightened sense of concern for the suffering of the thousands of others in the region. If another 'Vietnam' was in the offing then, at least this time, its progress would be universally challenged.

The Church's role
Even before the deaths of priests and nuns in Central America the Church was changing the perception of its role in Latin America. In the 1960s the Church emerged from centuries of accepting, even reinforcing, the ills of Latin American society to begin to re-examine its social, economic, and political attitudes. 'Liberation Theology', which was one outcome of this re-examination, saw many church-people repudiating the established role of the Church, which was to concentrate on salvation, preferring to work with and for the poor. Many were to press for radical solutions to the problems of the region. At the Conference of Latin American Bishops at Medellin, Colombia, in 1968 it was agreed that:

> 'Revolutionary insurrection may be legitimate in the case of evident and prolonged tyranny which dangerously threatens the common good of a country.'

61

In Nicaragua, priests, as well as the hierarchy of the Church, spoke out publicly against the crimes and abuses of Somoza. They joined the FSLN to fight actively for his overthrow. Some, like Ernesto Cardenal, were later to join the Government. Other priests are close to the people in the countryside. They share their poverty and, in countries like Guatemala and El Salvador, experience the injustices and terrors of daily life. 'Liberation Theology' has not gone unchallenged in the Church; Pope John Paul II has advised priests, like those in Nicaragua, to choose between their religious and secular duties.

World opinion

Outside the Church grave concern has been expressed by governments, as well as groups and individuals, about the

In the fighting against Somoza in the 1970s the Church played a constructive role. This priest, together with Red Cross workers, tried to bring about a cease fire in Matagalpa in 1978 in order to put a stop to the killing in Nicaragua's civil war.

situation in Central America. With the exception of the British government, led by Margaret Thatcher, who has a particularly close affinity to the politics of Ronald Reagan, European governments have advocated a political solution to the crisis in the region. Some, such as France and West Germany, have provided material support to countries like Nicaragua. The European Parliament stated 'that the problems of Central America cannot be solved by military means but only by a political solution springing from the region itself and respecting the principles of non-interference and inviolability of frontiers.'

The European Parliament also affirmed its support for the Contadora group of countries—Colombia, Mexico, Panama, and Venezuela, now supported by Argentina, Peru, Uruguay and Brazil—which took its name from the site of

A Soviet ship leaves Havana harbour. Cuba's strong links with the Soviet Union are a cause for concern to the United States.

the first meeting of the group on the Panamanian island of Contadora in January 1983. Their aim was to find a Latin American solution to the horrifying problems of the region which are setting Latin Americans against Latin Americans. The basic principles of the group are as follows: that force merely aggravates the underlying tensions; that peace can only be based upon non-intervention and self-determination; that there be equality among nations and co-operation for economic and social purposes; that disputes should be settled peacefully, and that there be free and authentic expression of the peoples' will. Despite considerable progress in securing the agreement of Central American countries to measures designed to achieve their objectives, further advances were brought to a halt by the United States which

effectively sabotaged the work of the group. Despite this setback most Latin American countries agree that the only way towards peace in Central America is through the Contadora, or similar, process.

The United States has attempted to link the crisis in Central America to Cuban and Soviet influence. Both countries have provided political support for opposition and guerrilla groups and, at different times, material assistance of varying kinds. Fidel Castro is reputed to have advised the Nicaraguans not to make the same mistakes made by the Cuban revolution in the 1960s. He advised maintaining the private sector in the economy, since it was both costly and unnecessary to abolish it. As the United States had the means, ultimately, to destroy the revolution, Castro advised caution in

all dealings with the US government. In a wider context Cuba, in the 1980s, supports a political settlement in Central America and plays a moderating role in dealing with guerilla groups

The Soviet Union has followed Cuba's example in providing Nicaragua with much-needed support, especially with weapons to defend its borders. However, the Soviet Union does not intend to provide Nicaragua with the high level of aid which it has given Cuba since 1959.

US foreign policy rarely affects domestic politics, and appears never to influence its presidential elections. If it did so it is unlikely that Ronald Reagan would have been re-elected President in 1984 when US public opinion was at its highest against the government's Central American policy. Since then, interest in the region declined, only to be brought back into focus with the 'Irangate' hearings in the summer of 1987.

9
Future perspectives

The signing of the Arias Peace Plan brought a new dimension into the Central American crisis but, as usual, the future depends on the United States. Could the election of a different US President bring about a change in policy? That would require an unprecedented U-turn with regard to America's relationship with, and attitude towards, Latin

Below *A Nicaraguan poster shows the different groups in society which support, and benefit from, 'the beautiful revolution' of the Sandinistas.*

Wounded Salvadorean
troops are evacuated
from the fighting zone
in the north east
where guerrilla groups
have established
strong bases.

America as a whole. The economic difficulties of the United States, caused by the world recession of the early 1980s, are likely to continue into the 1990s, making such a scenario unlikely especially in view of the vested business interests involved.

The United Nations has attempted to mediate in the area but without any success. The positioning of a UN peacekeeping force on, say, Nicaragua's borders could take some of the tension out of the region but, to date, has not been regarded as an acceptable option. There is a minority in the US government and military who would prefer a military solution in Central America, that is to say an invasion of Nicaragua. Such an option has always existed, but at such

astronomical economic and political cost that the United States has chosen not to bear it. In the meantime, the US government hopes to 'contain' Nicaragua, and to hold back its development, through its support of the *Contras*, although there is no evidence to suggest any real threat to the continued survival of the Sandinistas. Nor is it likely that the US government is any closer to accepting their presence in Central America, for, in nearly thirty years of existence, the United States is still unable to accept the permanence of Fidel Castro and the Cuban revolution.

The Central American peace agreement gave all concerned the best opportunity to solve the crisis. The agreement contained a number of points. Among them that there should be a ceasefire throughout Central America, that there should be a move towards more democratic political structures, and that all foreign interference and arms supplies should cease. The agreement was not endorsed by President Reagan, who had put forward his own plan, directed at Nicaragua. While the Sandinista government in Nicaragua began taking steps in accordance with the agreement, Reagan continued to pursue military aid for the Contras. His action demonstrated that despite the resolve within Central America for peace, foreign interference remains the main obstacle.

Above *Guatemalan President Vinicio Cerezo, on his way to Mass after signing the peace agreement with the other Presidents of Central American countries in August 1987.*

Date chart

1823 Monroe Doctrine declared by US President, claiming Latin America and the Caribbean as an area of US influence, off bounds for further European colonization.

1840s Gold prospectors cross Central America through Nicaragua on the way to the Californian gold fields.

1850 Clayton-Bulwer Treaty signed between the United States and Great Britain to end their rivalry over Central America.

1898 The United States invades Cuba and Puerto Rico.

1903 Panama Canal built.

1905 US troops land in Honduras.

1908 US troops sent to Panama.

1909 US Marines land at Bluefields in Nicaragua.

1912 Further US Marines land in Nicaragua.

1914 'Roosevelt Corollary' to the Monroe Doctrine of 1823; now it is the 'duty' of the United States to expand.

1914–34 US Marines occupy Haiti.

1925 US troops withdrawn from Nicaragua.

1926 US troops return to Nicaragua.

1927 Nicaraguan National Guard organized by US forces in Nicaragua.

1931 US Marines withdrawn from Nicaragua.

1933 US President Roosevelt declares his 'Good Neighbour Policy.'

1934 February 21st. Augusto Cesar Sandino shot in cold blood by the Nicaraguan National Guard.

1936 Anastasio Somoza seizes power in Nicaragua.

1954 US-organized invasion of Guatemala.

1959 Fidel Castro enters Havana; Cuban revolution begins.

1961 Bay of Pigs invasion; US-organized invasion defeated within 72 hours.

1962 Cuban Missile Crisis.

1965 US Marines invade the Dominican Republic.

1966 Death Squads appear in Guatemala; 20,000 deaths 1966–76.

1972 Managua earthquake, Nicaragua.

1976 US Congress Hearings on Human Rights in El Salvador, Guatemala and Nicaragua.

1977 Panama Canal Treaty signed limiting US control of the Panama Canal Zone.

1978 Civil War in Nicaragua as the people take to the streets to oust Somoza.

1979 Sandinistas topple Somoza in Nicaragua.

1979 New Jewel Movement led by Maurice Bishop ousts Eric Gairy in Grenada.

1980 President Reagan elected.

1980 March. Archbishop Romero assassinated.

1980 December. US missionaries murdered in El Salvador.

1981 President Reagan inaugurated. US aid to Nicaragua suspended; US military aid to El Salvador increased.

1981 Belize becomes independent.

1984 Elections in Nicaragua; Sandinistas receive overwhelming majority vote.

1986 International Court in the Hague deems US policy towards Nicaragua 'illegal'.

1987 August. Guatemala meeting of Central American Heads of State sign Central American Peace Agreement.

1987 August. President Reagan asks Congress for $270 million interim aid for the 'Contras'.

Glossary

Alliance for Progress This was formed in the 1960s by President John Kennedy to fend off 'other Cuban Revolutions' and bring about social reforms in Central, and Latin, America. The Alliance failed dismally, with US Aid benefitting vicious and corrupt regimes.

Central Intelligence Agency (CIA) The US government organization originally set up for intelligence gathering; recent evidence shows the CIA involved in illegal activities around the world, including drug-dealing, gunrunning, bomb outrages, and assassinations.

Clayton-Bulwer Treaty (1850) An attempt to defuse the rivalry over Central America existing between the US and Great Britain.

Contadora An island off Panama which gives its name to the group of Latin American countries seeking a political solution to the turmoil in Central America.

Contras The name given to Nicaraguan counter-revolutionaries, many of them former National Guard under Somoza, attacking Nicaragua from Honduras and Costa Rica.

Cuban Missile Crisis This took place in 1962, when the US blockaded Cuba in order to force the Soviet Union to dismantle its nuclear missile base.

Death Squads Right-wing groups in El Salvador and Guatemala which have systematically assassinated people consider to be the 'opposition'; these have included teachers, students, women and children.

Democratic Revolutionary Front (FDR) The broad front of political parties, labour federations and popular movements opposing the Salvadorean government and linked with the FMLN guerrillas.

Farabundo Marti National Liberation organisation (FMLN) The coalition of revolutionary guerrilla groups in El Salvador.

Good Neighbour Policy US policy towards Central and Latin America announced by President Roosevelt in 1933.

Gunboat Diplomacy Term given to repeated US military interventions and occupations in Central America and the Caribbean early in the 20th century.

Irangate/Contragate   The name given by the press to the US scandal involving profits from arms sold to Iran being given to the Contras.

Liberation Theology   The new attitude on the part of the Catholic Church which emphasizes the needs of the poor.

National Guard   Nicaraguan private army of the Somoza family until 1979.

Sandinista Front for National Liberation (FSLN)   The revolutionary organization which overthrew Anastasio Somoza in 1979 and took power in Nicaragua.

Vietnam War   The war fought by the US government against Vietnam from the 1960s to 1975 when US forces finally left Vietnam.

Further reading

ANGEL, A., and MACINTOSH, F. *The Tiger's Milk; Women of Nicaragua*, (Virago, 1987.)

BLACK, G. *Triumph of the People; the Sandinista revolution in Nicaragua*, (Zed Press, 1981.)

CABEZAS, O. *Fire From the Mountain; the making of a Sandinista*, Cape, 1986.

COXSEDGE, J. *Thank God for the Revolution; a journey through Central America* (Pluto, 1987.)

DIXON, M. and JONAS, S. Eds *Nicaragua Under Siege* (Synthesis Publications, 1984.)

DUNKERLEY, J. *The Long War; Dictatorship and Revolution in El Salvador*, (Junction Books, 1982.)

GRIFFITHS, J. *The Cuban Missile Crisis* (Wayland, 1986.)

EDWARDS, R. *The Vietnam War* (Wayland, 1986.)

KISSINGER, H. *The Report on the President's National Bipartisan Commission on Central America* (Macmillan, 1983.)

LATIN AMERICAN BUREAU, *Honduras; State for Sale* (LAB, 1987.)

MEISELAS, S. *Nicaragua* (Writers and Readers, 1981.)

PEARCE, JENNY *Under The Eagle* (Latin American Bureau, 1982.)

WEBER, H. *Nicaragua; The Sandinista Revolution* (Verso Books, 1983.)

WOODWARD, R. L. *Central America* (Oxford University Press, 1985.)

Index

Picture Acknowledgements

The publishers would like to thank the following for the loan of their photographs in this book: Camera Press frontispiece, 20, 21, 24, 26, 34, 37, 39, 51, 52, 58, 67, 68; John Griffiths 64, 70; Popperfoto 9, 10, 11, 12, 17, 18, 22, 29, 30, 32, 41, 49, 60, 62, 71; Rex Features COVER. The cartoon on p. 55 is by Roger Sanchez. The maps on pages 14, 16, 31, 40, 47 are by Malcolm S. Walker.